PHYSICAL SCIENCE

SORTING THE ELEMENTS

The Periodic Table at Work

Ian Barber

ROURKE PUBLISHING

Vero Beach, Florida 32964

www.rourkepublishing.com

PHOTO CREDITS: p. 37: Scott Barbour/Getty Images; p. 27: Soile Berg/istockphoto.com; p. 36 bottom: Lester V. Bergman/Corbis; pp. 18, 19, 24: Corbis; p. 35: U.S. Department of Defense; p. 5: Robert Estall/Corbis; p. 29: Dawne Fahey/EASI-Images/CFWImages.com; p. 40: Peter Ginter/Science Faction/Getty Images; p. 31: Pascal Goegheluck/Science Photo Library; p. 16: Hazlan Abdul Hakim/istockphoto.com; p. 33: Stephen Hoerold/ istockphoto.com; pp. 8, 10: Hulton Archive/Getty Images; p. 21: istockphoto.com; p. 39: Adam Korzekwa/istockphoto.com; p. 17: Andrew Lambert Photography/Science Photo Library; p. 36 top: Rich Lord/istockphoto.com; p. 11: National Optical Astronomy Observatories/Science Photo Library; p. 25: NASA; p. 34: Jane Norton/ istockphoto.com; p. 4: Chris Pollack/istockphoto.com; p. 28: J. C. Revy/Science Photo Library; p. 13: RGB Ltd/element-collection.com; p. 30: Nick Stubbs/istockphoto.com; p. 9: Sheila Terry/Science Photo Library; p. 12: Time & Life Pictures/Getty Images.

Cover picture shows a pile of sulfur powder.
[Charles D. Winters/Science Photo Library]

Produced for Rourke Publishing by Discovery Books
Editors: Geoff Barker, Amy Bauman, Rebecca Hunter
Designer: Ian Winton
Cover designer: Keith Williams
Illustrator: Stefan Chabluk
Photo researcher: Rachel Tisdale

Library of Congress Cataloging-in-Publication Data

Barber, Ian.
  Sorting the elements : the periodic table at work / Ian Barber.
      p. cm. -- (Let's explore science)
  Includes index.
  ISBN 978-1-60044-607-8 (Hard cover)
  ISBN 978-1-60694-994-8 (Soft cover)
  1. Chemical elements--Juvenile literature. 2. Periodic law--Tables--Juvenile literature. I. Title.
  QD466.B295 2008
  546'.8--dc22
                          2007020160

www.rourkepublishing.com - rourke@rourkepublishing.com
Post Office Box 643328 Vero Beach, Florida 32964

CONTENTS

chapter one

Elements and Atoms

What is an **element**? Elements are all around us. The element iron is in everything from bridges to safety pins. Electric wire is made from the element copper. Cans are made from the element aluminum. The lead in pencils is not really lead. It is graphite. This is the element carbon. Even the air we breathe is made of elements. It is mostly nitrogen and oxygen.

▲ *These wires are made from the element copper. Copper is a metal. It is used for wires because it conducts electricity well.*

▲*Ironbridge is built mainly from the element iron. It was the first bridge ever to be built of cast iron. It was built across the River Severn in England, in 1779.*

But many things around us are not elements. Plastic is not an element. Wood, glass, and cloth are not elements, either. So how do we tell elements from other substances? To find the answer, let's look at **atoms**. Everything is made of atoms.

Atoms and Elements

Atoms are the bits, or particles, that make up everything. They are very tiny. You need a special microscope to see an atom. An element is something that is made up of just one kind of atom.

ATOMIC STRUCTURE

Atoms are not solid balls. They are made from smaller parts. The parts are **protons**, **neutrons**, and **electrons**. The middle of the atom is called the **nucleus**. It is made from protons and neutrons. Around this is a cloud of very, very tiny electrons. The various elements have a different number of protons, neutrons, and electrons.

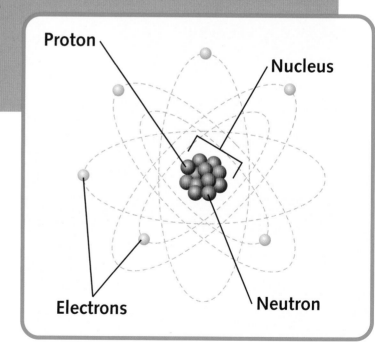

Proton

Nucleus

Electrons

Neutron

▶ *The main parts of an atom.*

How Many Elements Are There?

About ninety-two elements have been found on Earth. Some others have been made artificially. (See page 19.)

ELEMENT SYMBOLS

Every element has a symbol. Often, it is the first one or two letters of the element's name. Carbon, for instance, is C. Oxygen is O, and aluminum is Al. Sometimes, the symbol is not so easy to figure out. Iron, for example, is Fe. This symbol comes from the Latin name for iron, which is ferrum.

Element	Symbol	Element	Symbol
aluminum	Al	nickel	Ni
arsenic	As	nitrogen	N
carbon	C	oxygen	O
chlorine	Cl	phosphorus	P
cobalt	Co	platinum	Pt
copper	Cu	potassium	K
fluorine	F	silicon	Si
gold	Au	silver	Ag
helium	He	sodium	Na
hydrogen	H	sulfur	S
iodine	I	tin	Sn
iron	Fe	titanium	Ti
magnesium	Mg	uranium	U
mercury	Hg	zinc	Zn

chapter two

Discovering the Elements

It took a long time for scientists to understand what elements are. Ancient Greeks such as Aristotle thought that there were only four elements—air, fire, earth, and water. For many years, most people believed these ideas.

►*This picture from 1545 shows an alchemist at work. He is using a furnace to heat a water bath.*

But then came Robert Boyle, an Irish chemist. In the 1650s, he proved that there are many elements, not just four. Then in 1789, French chemist Antoine Lavoisier made the first list of elements. The list included the elements known at the time. Among them were light and heat. We now know these are not elements. Lavoisier also defined what an element is. He said it is a substance that can not be broken down into simpler substances.

▲ *A picture of Antoine Lavoisier in his laboratory. He is doing an experiment to try and separate water into its elements.*

ALCHEMISTS

Until the 17th century, most people who studied chemistry were **alchemists**. Alchemists worked with elements like today's chemists do. But they used them to try to turn one substance into another. Turning common metal into gold is one example. It didn't work, and it sounds funny now. But they made useful scientific discoveries along the way.

More and More Elements

Lavoisier's work helped show what an element was. After that, more were discovered. Many of them were found using new methods. For example, the first battery was made in 1800. Chemists found a good use for it. They discovered that they could use electricity to separate many substances into their elements.

▲*Humphry Davy was one of the first scientists to discover new elements using batteries. He discovered six elements (sodium, potassium, magnesium, calcium, strontium, and barium) this way.*

Chemists also discovered new elements by looking at the light that substances gave off as they burned. Gustave Kirchoff and Robert Bunsen were German chemists. They used a **prism** to split the light coming from a burning object. Then they looked at the lines that were produced (called a **spectrum**). The method is known as **spectroscopy**. Bunsen and Kirchoff discovered the elements cesium and rubidium this way.

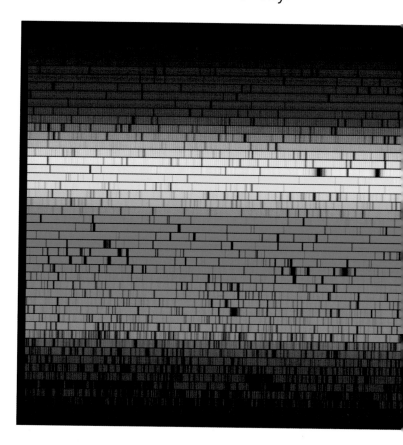

▶ *This image shows a spectrum of light coming from the star "Arcturus." Scientists are able to tell what elements the star is made of by the position of the dark lines.*

Elements in the Sun

Spectroscopy was also used to look at the light from the Sun and stars. Scientists Joseph Lockyer and Pierre Janssen did this. In 1868, they looked at the Sun's spectrum during an eclipse. They found lines for an element they did not know. The new element was called helium. Later, scientists found helium on Earth, too.

Mendeleev's Table

By the 1860s, chemists had named more than sixty elements. Some of these, they saw, had things in common. They had similar properties. The elements could be grouped by these. Was there a pattern to the groups? The answer came in 1869. It came from a Russian chemist Dmitri Mendeleev.

Mendeleev wrote the name of each element on a card. That way, he could rearrange them. He put the elements in order of their **atomic weight**. He made a few changes and grouped together elements with similar properties.

▶ *This photo shows Mendeleev working in his study.*

ATOMIC WEIGHT

Atoms of different elements have different masses, or weights. So how do we measure an element's atomic mass (weight)? It is the weight of a certain amount of that element compared to the weight of the same amount of another element.

Mendeleev made a table of elements showing the groups he saw. This is known as the **periodic table**. When he made the table, he left gaps. These marked places where Mendeleev thought an element was missing. He was sure some had not been discovered yet. He was right. Elements discovered since now fill the gaps.

▶ This picture shows a large lump of the chemical element, gallium. It is one of the elements that Mendeleev rightly predicted would be discovered in the future.

chapter three

Rows and Columns

The periodic table shows the elements by atomic mass. The table starts with the lightest element. And it ends with the heaviest. Hydrogen is the lightest element. It has one proton and one electron. Next is helium. It has two protons and two electrons. Lithium has three protons and electrons, and so on. (The number of protons or electrons in an element's atom is called its **atomic number**.)

▶ *A helium atom has a nucleus with two protons and two neutrons. Two electrons zoom around the nucleus.*

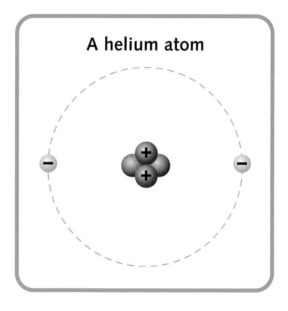

A helium atom

The periodic table has seven rows. (See pages 42-43.) Each row holds a different number of elements. The first row has two elements—hydrogen and helium. The next two rows have eight elements each. (Elements 57-70 and 89-102 are very similar. They are often put in a separate block at the bottom.)

OTHER PERIODIC TABLES

The periodic table is often shown in rows and columns. But, there are many ways to show it. There are circular versions and spiral versions. Some are shown in three dimensions or as a chemical galaxy.

Circular Periodic Table

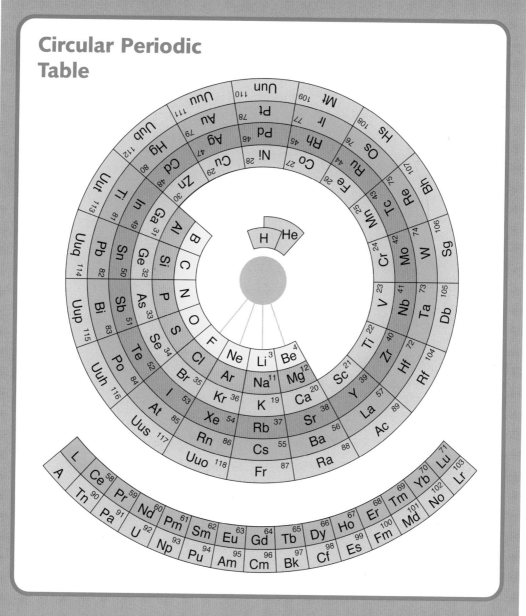

▲*Diamond is the strongest natural material found on Earth. This drill bit is made of diamond. It is used in the oil industry to drill through rock.*

Looking at the Groups

Look at the periodic table on pages 42-43. Each column is a group of elements. They have properties that are similar. Properties are things like melting point, boiling point, hardness or softness, or whether an element is **reactive** or not.

The elements in Group 1, for example, are soft metals. They melt at a low temperature. When they burn, they have a colored flame. These elements also react quickly. Potassium, for example, catches fire and burns if it touches water. It is stored in oil to avoid this.

RECORD-BREAKING ELEMENTS

Hardest element:	carbon (diamond)
Densest element:	osmium
Lightest element:	hydrogen
Highest melting point:	tungsten at 6,192°F (3,422°C).
Lowest freezing point:	helium (It does not freeze even at very low temperatures.)

▲Putting the element potassium in water is dangerous. It fizzes, smokes, then starts to burn with a purple flame.

Discovering the Noble Gases

Mendeleev's periodic table was missing a whole group of elements. This was Group 18. (See pages 42-43.) The elements of this group are very different from those in Group 1. They are colorless gases. They do not react with other elements. These are the **noble gases**. When Mendeleev created the table, none of these gases had been discovered. Since they do not react with anything, they were hard to identify.

In 1894, the Scottish chemist William Ramsay discovered the first noble gas. It was argon. Ramsay saw that it did not fit with the table's other groups. He suggested there must be a whole group of these gases. He was right. The others were discovered over the next six years.

▶ *Although noble gases are colorless, they can produce very bright colors. Most of the lights in this city street have a small amount of a noble gas in them. When electricity passes through the gas, it glows brightly. Different noble gases produce different colors.*

NEW ELEMENTS

Ninety-two different elements are found on Earth. But the periodic table shows **118** elements. The extra elements have been made by scientists in the laboratory. Some may exist for only a moment.

Common Elements

There are ninety-two elements found on Earth. But only a few are very common. Most elements are found only in small quantities.

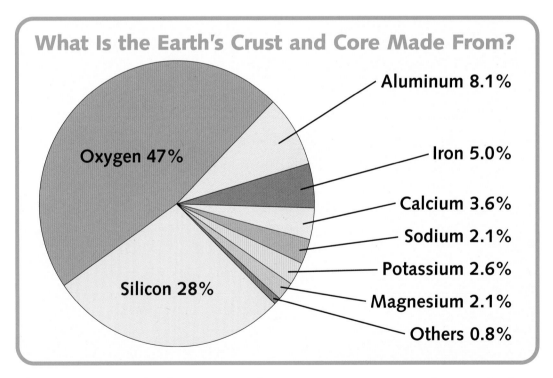

What Is the Earth's Crust and Core Made From?

Oxygen 47%

Silicon 28%

Aluminum 8.1%

Iron 5.0%

Calcium 3.6%

Sodium 2.1%

Potassium 2.6%

Magnesium 2.1%

Others 0.8%

▲ *Oxygen and silicon are the most common elements in the ground. This is because many rocks are made mainly of a substance called silicon dioxide. This substance is a combination of silicon and oxygen.*

Earth Elements

The ground beneath our feet is made mostly from just eight elements. They are oxygen, silicon, aluminum, iron, calcium, sodium, potassium, and magnesium. Many rocks are made from a mix of silicon and oxygen. Rocks such as chalk are mostly calcium and oxygen. Metals such as iron and aluminum are found in rocks called **ores**. The Earth's core is mostly iron.

Water Elements

The main elements in the ocean are hydrogen and oxygen. These are the elements that make water. Sodium and chlorine are found in small amounts in seawater. They make the sea salty. Other elements are found in small amounts, too. These include sulfur, magnesium, calcium, and potassium.

▲ *The 92 elements found on Earth combine together in different ways. They make up the air in the atmosphere, the water in the sea, and the rocks beneath us.*

Air Elements

Air is nearly 99 percent nitrogen and oxygen. Another 1 percent is argon. There are also small amounts of other gases in it. Carbon dioxide is one of them.

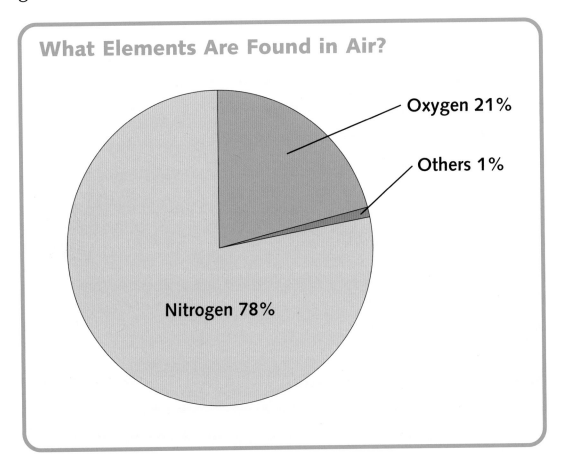

What Elements Are Found in Air?

Oxygen 21%

Others 1%

Nitrogen 78%

ESSENTIAL ELEMENT

Magnesium is important to all life. How? All living things depend on plants. Plants can make their own food from sunlight. The green color in plants is chlorophyll. This is the main substance for absorbing light. Magnesium is an essential part of chlorophyll.

Elements of Life

All living things are made up of just a few elements. For example, all living things have a great deal of water. Oxygen and hydrogen make water. So they are important elements. Other important elements include carbon and nitrogen. Animals and plants also need small amounts of several other elements. Two of these are calcium and iron. In humans, calcium is an important element for teeth and bones. And iron is needed for the blood.

▶ *94 percent of the human body is made up of the key elements oxygen, carbon, and hydrogen.*

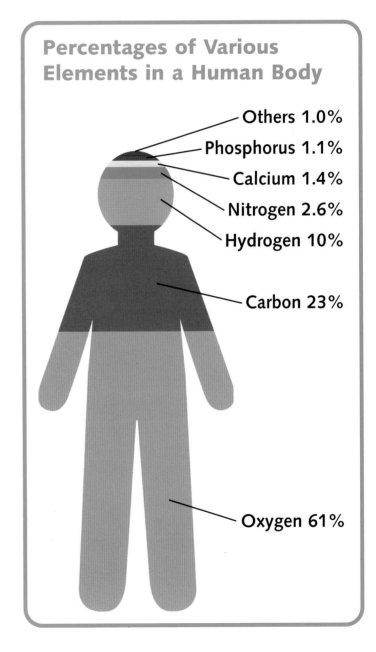

Percentages of Various Elements in a Human Body

Others 1.0%

Phosphorus 1.1%

Calcium 1.4%

Nitrogen 2.6%

Hydrogen 10%

Carbon 23%

Oxygen 61%

Elements in Space

On Earth, oxygen is the most common element. Beyond Earth the most common element is hydrogen. More than 92 percent of the universe is hydrogen. Most of the rest is helium. Other elements make up only about one ten-thousandth of the universe.

Hydrogen is also found in stars. Stars are huge balls of it. This is the fuel that keeps them burning. Also, huge clouds of hydrogen gas float in space.

▲ *Our Sun is just one of billions and billions of stars in the universe. Every one of these stars is made mostly of the element hydrogen.*

ELEMENT FACTORIES

Stars burn hydrogen. It is converted into elements such as carbon, oxygen, nitrogen, and iron. A few giant stars make elements that are heavier than iron. The heaviest elements, such as gold and uranium, are made in explosions called **supernovas**. These happen when a large star comes to the end of its life.

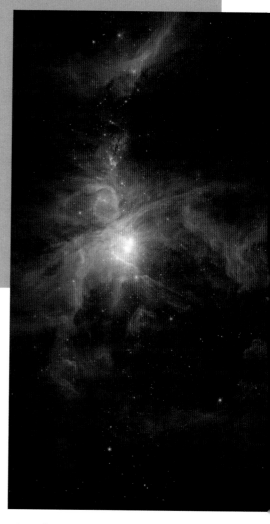

▲ This photo of the Orion nebula shows reddish clouds of hydrogen.

The fourteen most common elements in the universe

1	hydrogen	10,000,000
2	helium	1,400,000
3	oxygen	6,800
4	carbon	3,000
5	neon	2,800
6	nitrogen	910
7	magnesium	290
8	silicon	250
9	sulfur	95
10	iron	80
11	argon	42
12	aluminum	19
13	sodium	17
14	calcium	17
	all other elements	50

◀ The table shows the number of atoms of each element per 10 million hydrogen atoms.

Metals

The periodic table can be divided into two main types of elements. These are metals and nonmetals. Most elements are metals.

Metals in the Periodic Table

3 Li	4 Be															
11 Na	12 Mg												13 Al			
19 K	20 Ca	21 Sc	22 Ti	23 V	24 Cr	25 Mn	26 Fe	27 Co	28 Ni	29 Cu	30 Zn	31 Ga				
37 Rb	38 Sr	39 Y	40 Zr	41 Nb	42 Mo	43 Tc	44 Ru	45 Rh	46 Pd	47 Ag	48 Cd	49 In	50 Sn		
55 Cs	56 Ba	71 Lu	72 Hf	73 Ta	74 W	75 Re	76 Os	77 Ir	78 Pt	79 Au	80 Hg	81 Ti	82 Pb	83 Bi	
87 Fr	88 Ra	103 Lr	104 Rf	105 Db	106 Sg	107 Bh	108 Hs	109 Mt	110 Uun	111 Uuu	112 Uub	113 Uut	114 Uuq	115 Uup	

X naturally occurring elements

X synthetic elements

57 La	58 Ce	59 Pr	60 Nd	61 Pm	62 Sm	63 Eu	64 Gd	65 Tb	66 Dy	67 Ho	68 Er	69 Tm	70 Yb
89 Ac	90 Th	91 Pa	92 U	93 Np	94 Pu	95 Am	96 Cm	97 Bk	98 Cf	99 Es	100 Fm	101 Md	102 No

▲ *This shows only the metals in the periodic table.*

Metals conduct electricity and heat. Many are strong, shiny materials. They are often hard to melt. But, not all metals are like this. Some, such as sodium and potassium, are soft. Mercury is a metal, too. It is liquid at room temperature.

Many metals are malleable. This means they can be shaped. They can be bent or hammered into new shapes without breaking. Some are also ductile. This means they can be drawn out to make a thin wire.

▶ *This blacksmith is hammering an iron bar to shape it. The end of the bar is red hot, because heating the iron makes it softer and easier to shape.*

ALLOYS

An alloy is a metal-based mixture. It can be made by mixing two metals together. It can also be made by adding a small amount of nonmetal to a metal. The properties of alloys are different from the pure metals they are made from. For example, iron rusts easily. Chromium is not strong. However, if you alloy (mix) iron with at least 10 percent chromium you get stainless steel. This material is strong and does not rust.

Metal Reactions

Metals have some chemical properties in common. For instance, all metals form **salts** when they combine with **acids**. Sodium will react with the acid hydrogen chloride to make sodium chloride (table salt). The reaction is dangerous. It happens fast and produces lots of heat.

Table salt is only one of many salts. Epsom salt, for instance, is a medicine that helps heal scratches and rashes. It is a salt of the metal magnesium. Cinnabar is a reddish kind of rock. It is a salt of mercury. In the past, cinnabar was used to make vermilion, a brilliant red paint.

When an acid and a metal react together, they produce another substance besides a salt. The other product is hydrogen gas.

▶ *Cinnabar is a salt containing mercury and sulphur (HgS). It is the most common ore of mercury.*

RUSTY METALS

Most metals react with oxygen. They form substances called **oxides**. Iron reacts with oxygen in the air. It results in a reddish, powdery oxide, better known as rust. Other metals "rust" in air, too. But, in some metals, such as aluminum, the oxide forms a thin, hard coating on the surface. This coating protects the metal from further "rusting."

▲ *This truck has reached the end of its life and is covered in rust. The paint on a car or truck protects the steel body from rust for years. Other steel or iron parts of the car are covered with a thin layer of zinc to stop them from rusting.*

Different Metals

Different metals have things in common. But, there are many differences between them, too.

Copper is a good **conductor** of electricity. It is often used for electric wires. Iron is very strong. So iron and steel are often used to build skyscrapers, bridges, and other structures. Aluminum is strong, too. It is lighter than iron. It is used in structures that need to be both light and strong, such as airplane frames. Iron, cobalt, and nickel are the only elements that are magnetic. They are used to make magnets.

▶*Copper conducts heat as well as electricity. This is why these pans are made from copper.*

Some alloys (metal mixtures) have special properties, too. Bismuth alloys melt in hot water, like chocolate. Certain alloys are called memory metals. These can be treated so that they "remember" their shape. If the alloy is bent or twisted, it can be heated. Then it will return to its original shape.

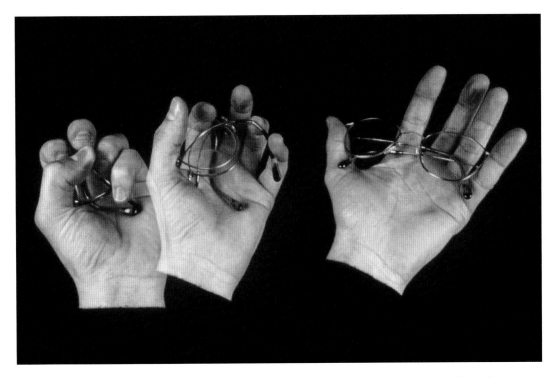

▲ *These spectacles are made from memory metal. The metal bends when it is squashed, but afterwards the frames spring back to their original shape.*

AMAZING METALS

Some metals have interesting properties. Mercury is a liquid at room temperature. Potassium and lithium catch fire in water. Gold can be beaten into a sheet four-hundred times thinner than a human hair.

chapter six

Nonmetals

There are eighteen nonmetals. Twelve are gases. Five are solids. One (bromine) is a liquid. Nonmetals are a varied group. But they do have some things in common. They are **insulators** rather than conductors. This means electricity and heat do not easily pass through them. Solid nonmetals are rigid. If you shape or stretch them, they break. Nonmetals do not form salts with acids.

Nonmetals and Metalloids

1 H					2 He
5 B	6 C	7 N	8 O	9 F	10 Ne
	14 Si	15 P	16 S	17 Cl	18 Ar
	32 Ge	33 As	34 Se	35 Br	36 Kr
		51 Sb	52 Te	53 I	54 Xe
			84 Po	85 At	86 Rn
			116 Uuh	117 Uus	118 Uuo

X naturally occurring elements   X synthetic elements

◄ The elements colored pink in this section of the periodic table are nonmetals.

Nonmetals are more common than metals. Nine of the ten most common elements in the universe are nonmetals.

NOT QUITE METALS

One small group of elements is very interesting. They are not quite metals or nonmetals. They are called **metalloids**. (These are colored blue in the table on page 32.) Some metalloids, such as silicon, are semiconductors. This means they are poor conductors of electricity when they are pure. However, when small amounts of other materials are added, they can conduct electricity. Silicon and other semiconductors are the basis of microchips and other electronic devices.

▲*Microchips are made mostly from silicon and other semiconductors. Hundreds of identical chips are made all together on a thin sheet of very pure silicon.*

▲ *At one time airships were filled with hydrogen, because it is the lightest gas. However, there were a few terrible accidents in which airships burned up. Helium is used in modern airships because it does not burn.*

Common Gases

Only nonmetals are gases. The most common one is hydrogen. It is the simplest element and the lightest gas. At one time, hydrogen was used in balloons and airships. But, hydrogen can burn quickly. For safety, helium is now used instead. It is almost as light as hydrogen, but it is unreactive.

THE HALOGENS

The halogens are elements in Group 17 of the periodic table. (See pages 42-43.) Fluorine and chlorine are reactive gases. Bromine is a liquid, and iodine is a solid. Fluorine is so reactive that chemists have been able to make it react with the noble gas xenon. No other element can be made to combine with a noble gas.

Oxygen is the most common element on Earth. About a fifth of the air is oxygen. Without oxygen, nothing could live. Nothing would burn. The other four-fifths of the air is nearly all nitrogen. Like helium, nitrogen is not reactive. Reactive substances such as explosives are often stored in nitrogen for safety.

▲*Most aircraft fly so high that the air is too thin for breathing. The pilot has to take a supply of oxygen to breathe at high altitude.*

Solids

The most important solid nonmetal is carbon. Carbon is found in two different forms. It can form hard, clear diamonds or soft, gray graphite.

▶*Diamond (right) and graphite (below) are very different materials, but they are both pure carbon.*

Carbon is an important part of all living things. A huge variety of other substances, including coal, oil, and plastics, are also made mainly from carbon.

Phosphorus comes in three colors: white, red, and black. White phosphorus is a waxy solid that glows in the dark. It is used to make useful products, such as fertilizers, weed killers, and cleaning products. Sulfur is a soft yellow solid. In the past, it was used to **fumigate** houses. It can kill plant fungi. Today, sulfur is in all kinds of chemicals. It is used to harden rubber.

SMELLY STUFF

If something smells bad, it probably has sulfur in it. Stink bombs are usually made from sulfur chemicals. Some tropical flowers have a "rotting" smell that comes from sulfur. The chemicals in skunk spray, all contain sulfur. This may be the world's worst smell.

▶ *This giant flower is a titan arum, or corpse flower. When it opens the flower smells of rotting meat. The rotting smell comes from chemicals containing sulfur.*

chapter seven

Elements into Compounds

We have seen that Earth has only ninety-two elements. But there are millions of different substances. Most of these come from compounds. This means they are mixes of two or more different elements. Elements are the building blocks for compounds. A compound is made of two or more different atoms joined together.

Joining Up Atoms

There are many ways to join two or even three different elements together. Many common substances are simple compounds. Often they are made from just a few elements.

Water, for instance, is written as H_2O. This means that water **molecules** are made of two atoms of hydrogen joined to one atom of oxygen. Table salt is even simpler. It is the elements sodium and chlorine joined together—NaCl.

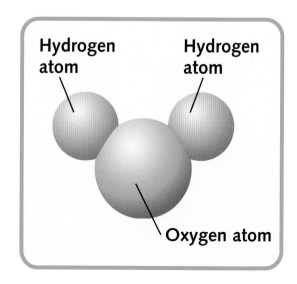

Hydrogen atom

Hydrogen atom

Oxygen atom

▶ *A molecule of water (H_2O).*

But some compounds are more complex than salt and water. In living things, compounds can have very large molecules. Proteins, for instance, can contain thousands of atoms.

BIGGEST MOLECULE

The biggest molecule is probably deoxyribonucleic acid, or DNA. DNA is what our genes are made from. In humans, a DNA molecule holds over thirteen billion atoms.

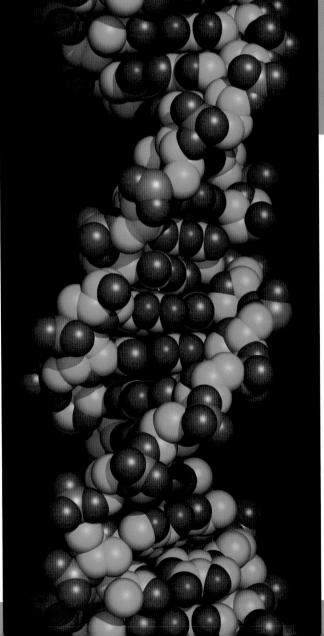

▶ This model shows a short section of a DNA molecule. It is made of two very long chains of atoms, twisted together in a spiral.

▲*As new kinds of technology develop, we find new ways of using elements. The wires being wound here are made from the elements titanium and niobium. They are used to make special magnets.*

Reacting With Other Elements

We have seen that some elements are reactive. Others are not. Potassium, for instance, reacts violently with water. The noble gases do not react with anything.

Scientists have found patterns in the reactivity of elements. Metals are more reactive the farther down the column, or group, you go. In Group 1, for example, potassium is more reactive than sodium and lithium. Nonmetals get less reactive as you move down the group. For example, fluorine is the most reactive of the halogens. Chlorine, which is below it, is less reactive.

Organizing Chemistry

Chemists can tell a lot about an element by looking at its place in the periodic table. They can tell if its atoms are large or small. They can tell if it is a metal or a nonmetal. They can get some idea of how reactive it is. They know what elements it might react with. By simply organizing the elements in a particular way, the periodic table helps to understand the whole of chemistry.

DANGEROUS IN WATER!

Potassium is in Group I of the periodic table. Group I elements are called alkaline metals. We have already seen that potassium bursts into flames if you put it in water. Potassium is not the most reactive alkaline metal, however. Rubidium and cesium are lower down Group I. When these elements are mixed with water, they explode! (Francium, which is below cesium in Group I, is radioactive and too unstable for chemical reactions.)

Full Periodic Table

All Metals, Nonmetals, and Metalloids

Group

	1	2		3	4	5	6	7	8
1	1 H								
2	3 Li	4 Be							
3	11 Na	12 Mg							
4	19 K	20 Ca		21 Sc	22 Ti	23 V	24 Cr	25 Mn	26 Fe
5	37 Rb	38 Sr		39 Y	40 Zr	41 Nb	42 Mo	43 Tc	44 Ru
6	55 Cs	56 Ba		71 Lu	72 Hf	73 Ta	74 W	75 Re	76 Os
7	87 Fr	88 Ra		103 Lr	104 Rf	105 Db	106 Sg	107 Bh	108 Hs

Period

☐ metals

☐ nonmetals

☐ metalloids

57 La	58 Ce	59 Pr	60 Nd	61 Pm	62 Sm
89 Ac	90 Th	91 Pa	92 U	93 Np	94 Pu

Group

9	10	11	12	13	14	15	16	17	18

									2 He
				5 B	6 C	7 N	8 O	9 F	10 Ne
				13 Al	14 Si	15 P	16 S	17 Cl	18 Ar
27 Co	28 Ni	29 Cu	30 Zn	31 Ga	32 Ge	33 As	34 Se	35 Br	36 Kr
45 Rh	46 Pd	47 Ag	48 Cd	49 In	50 Sn	51 Sb	52 Te	53 I	54 Xe
77 Ir	78 Pt	79 Au	80 Hg	81 Ti	82 Pb	83 Bi	84 Po	85 At	86 Rn
109 Mt	110 Uun	111 Uuu	112 Uub	113 Uut	114 Uuq	115 Uup	116 Uuh	117 Uus	118 Uuo

63 Eu	64 Gd	65 Tb	66 Dy	67 Ho	68 Er	69 Tm	70 Yb
95 Am	96 Cm	97 Bk	98 Cf	99 Es	100 Fm	101 Md	102 No

X naturally occurring elements

X synthetic elements

Glossary

acid (ASS id) — a substance that turns litmus paper red and makes salts with metals. Weak acids are sour-tasting, strong acids can burn.

alchemist (AL kur mist) — a type of ancient scientist who did chemical experiments to try and find the secret of eternal life, and how to turn other metals into gold

atomic number (uh TOM ik NUHM bur) — the number of protons or electrons that an atom of an element has

atomic weight (uh TOM ik wate) — the weight of an atom of an element compared to the weight an atom of another element, which is used as a standard. Carbon is used as the standard today. It is given an atomic weight of 12.

atoms (AT uhms) — extremely tiny particles that are the basic building blocks of all substances

conductor (kuhn DUHKT tur) — a substance that allows electricity or heat to pass through it easily

electron (i LEK tron) — a tiny particle with a negative electric charge. Electrons are parts of an atom.

element (EL uh muhnt) — a substance that is made up of just one kind of atom

fumigate (FYOO muh gate) — to treat with fumes to disinfect an area or get rid of pests

insulator (IN suh lay tur) — a substance that does not allow electricity or heat to pass through it easily

metalloids (MET uhl oids) — elements that are not metals, but have some similar properties to metals

molecule (MOL uh kyool) — a combination of two or more atoms, joined together by chemical bonds

neutron (NOO tron) — a tiny particle with no electric charge found in the nucleus of the atom

noble gases (NOH buhl GASS iz) — a group of elements, all gases, that do not react with other elements

nucleus (NOO klee uhss) — in chemistry, the nucleus is the central part of a atom

ore (or) — any kind of rock that is rich in a metal

oxide (OX ide) — a compound combining oxygen with one or more metallic elements

periodic table (pihr ee OD ik TAY buhl) — a way of arranging the elements so that elements with similar properties are grouped together

prism (PRIZ uhm) — a specially shaped piece of glass that can split light into separate colors

proton (PROH ton) — a tiny particle with a positive electric charge found in the nucleus of the atom

reactive (ree AK tiv) — an element is chemically reactive if it easily combines with other substances

salt (sawlt) — table salt, or sodium chloride, is the most common salt. Other salts are the result of a reaction between a metal and one or more nonmetals.

spectroscopy (SPEK tross kuh pee) — a way of finding what elements are in something that is glowing or burning, by looking at the spectrum of the light it gives off

spectrum (SPEK truhm) — the pattern of colors and dark areas you get when you split light with a prism

supernova (soo pur NOH vuh) — a massive explosion that happens when a very big star runs out of fuel

Further Information

Books

A History of Super Science: Atoms And Elements. Andrew Solway. Raintree, 2006.

Elements: What You Really Want to Know. Ron Miller. Twenty-First Century Books, 2006.

From Greek Atoms to Quarks: Discovering Atoms. Sally Morgan. Heinemann Library, 2007.

Periodic Table: Elements with Style! Adrian Dingle. Kingfisher Books, 2007.

Websites to visit

http://www.webelements.com/webelements/scholar/ index.html
Select any element from the periodic table to find out all about it.

http://www.nndc.bnl.gov/content/HistoryOfElements.html
National Nuclear Data Center
Who discovered chromium? How did dubnium get its name? You can find out all about the history of the elements on this website.

http://www.meta-synthesis.com/webbook/35_pt/pt.html
All kinds of ways that the periodic table has been organized, from simple tables to an element galaxy.

http://www.uky.edu/Projects/Chemcomics/
The Comic Book Periodic Table
Click on an element and find all the comic book pages that mention that element.

http://education.jlab.org/indexpages/elementgames.php
Jefferson Lab
This site offers an array of games and puzzles based on the elements.

http://elements.wlonk.com
This site provides a periodic table of the elements in pictures.

Index